EASY KEYBOARD AND PIANO PIECES

John Jester

30 Easy-to-play Pieces for Beginners

Easy Keyboard and Piano Pieces is the perfect companion for those starting out to learn the keyboard or piano. The book uses simple, popular and familiar tunes which helps the player feel more comfortable as they learn the easy-to-play pieces. All notes have their letters printed above them in a large easy-to-read font, to help those who are yet to learn how to read music. Also included are some blank music sheets, so you can have fun creating your own compositions.

Easy Keyboard and Piano Pieces is the ideal first music book.

CONTENTS

4	Twinkle, Twinkle
5	Are You Sleeping?
6	Baa, Baa, Black Sheep
7	The Wheels on the Bus
8	London Bridge
9	Good Morning to All
10	I'm a Little Teapot
11	Polly Put the Kettle On
12	Ring a Ring of Roses
13	The Grand Old Duke of York
14	Old McDonald
15	Oranges and Lemons
16	Three Blind Mice
17	Hickory, Dickory, Dock
18	Hot Cross Buns
19	Happy and You Know It
20	The Muffin Man
21	The Mulberry Bush
22	Sing a Song of Sixpence
23	Row Your Boat
24	Kumbaya
25	Itsy Bitsy Spider
26	Rudolph the Red-nosed Reindeer
27	Humpty Dumpty
28	Girls and Boys
29	Pop goes the weasel
30	Heads, Shoulders, Knees and Toes
31	Nellie the Elephant
32	Round the Mountain
33	I Am the Music Man
34-40	Write Your Own Composition

Twinkle, Twinkle

C C G G   A A G   F F E E

Twin-kle, twin-kle, lit-tle star. How I won-der

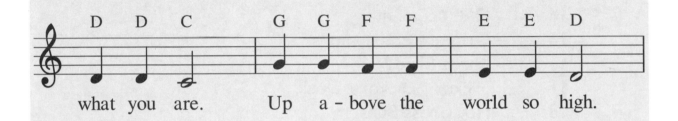

D D C   G G F F   E E D

what you are. Up a-bove the world so high.

G G F F E E D   C C G G

Like a dia-mond in the sky. Twin-kle, twin-kle

A A G   F F E E   D D C

lit-tle star. How I won-der what you are.

Are You Sleeping?

Baa, Baa, Black Sheep

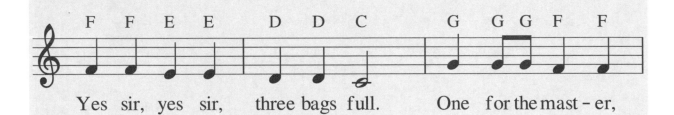

The Wheels on the Bus

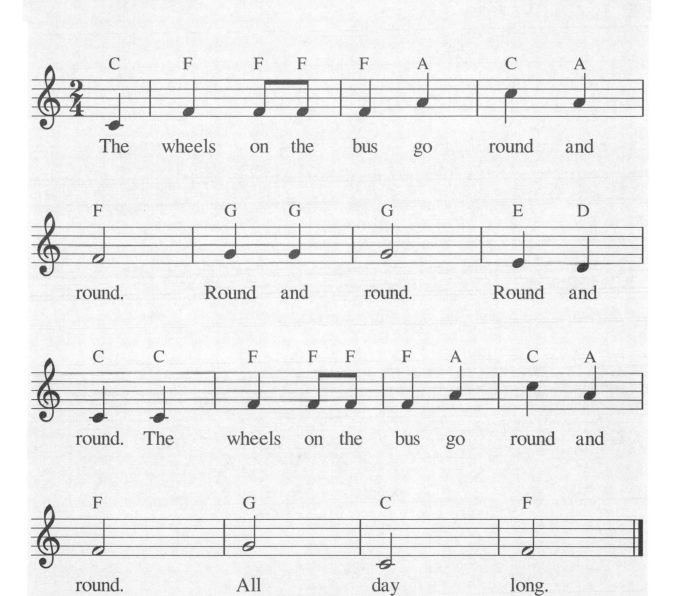

The wheels on the bus go round and round. Round and round. Round and round. The wheels on the bus go round and round. All day long.

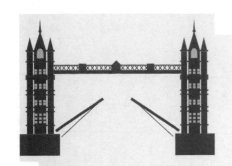

London Bridge

Lon - don Bridge is   fall - ing down.   Fall - ing down,

fall - ing down.   Lon - don Bridge is   fall - ing down,

My   fair   la - dy.

Good Morning to All

Good   morn-ing   to   you,   Good   morn-ing   to

you.   Good   morn - ing   dear   chil - dren,   Good

morn - ing   to   you.

I'm a Little Teapot

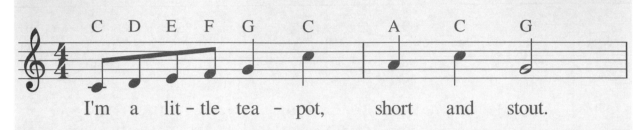

I'm a lit - tle tea - pot, short and stout.

Here's my han – dle, here's my spout.

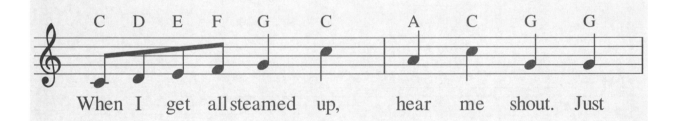

When I get all steamed up, hear me shout. Just

tip me o – ver and pour me out.

Polly Put the Kettle On

Ring a Ring of Roses

Ring a ring of ro - ses. A poc-ket full of po - sies. A -

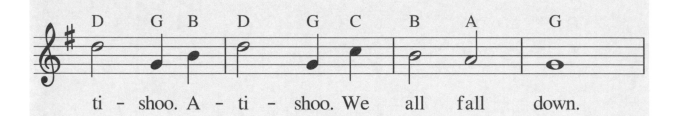

ti - shoo. A - ti - shoo. We all fall down.

Ring a ring of ro - ses. A poc-ket full of po - sies. A -

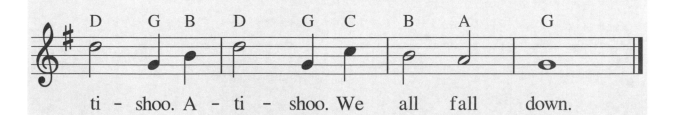

ti - shoo. A - ti - shoo. We all fall down.

The Grand Old Duke of York

The grand old Duke of York. He had ten thou-sand men. He marched them up to the top of the hill, and he marched them down a - gain. And when they were up, they were up. And when they were down, they were down. And when they were on - ly half way up, they were nei - ther up nor down.

Old McDonald

C C C G A A G   E E D D C   G

Old Mc-Don-ald   had a farm.   E I E I O.   And

C C C G A A G   E E D D C   G G

on his farm he   had a cow.   E I E I O.   With a

C C C G G C C C

moo moo here and a moo moo there.

C C C C C C   C C C C C C

Here a moo, there a moo,   ev-ery-where a moo moo.

C C C G A A G   E E D D C

Old Mc-Don-ald   had a farm.   E I E I O.

Oranges and Lemons

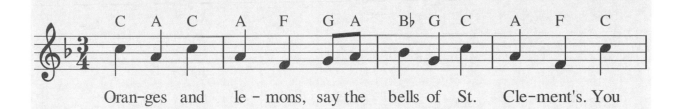

Oran-ges and le-mons, say the bells of St. Cle-ment's. You

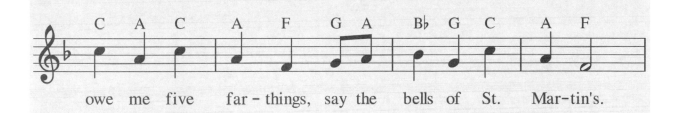

owe me five far-things, say the bells of St. Mar-tin's.

When will you pay me? Say the bells of Old Bai-ley.

When I grow rich, say the bells of Shore-ditch.

Three Blind Mice

E	D	C	E	D	C	G	F	F	E

Three blind mice.   Three blind mice.   See   how they run.

G	F	F	E	G	C	C	B	A	B	C	G	G	G

See   how they run.   They   all   ran   af-ter the   farm-er's   wife, who

C	C	C	B	A	B	C	G	G	G	G

cut   off   their   tails   with   a   carv – ing   knife.   Have you

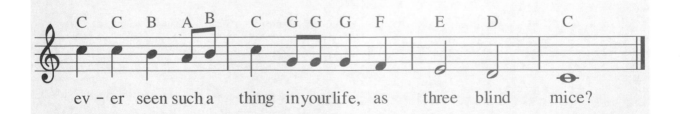

C	C	B	A	B	C	G	G	G	F	E	D	C

ev – er   seen such a   thing in your life, as   three   blind   mice?

Hickory, Dickory, Dock

Hick – or – y, Dick – or – y, Dock. The

mouse ran up the clock. The

clock struck one. The mouse ran down.

Hick – or – y, Dick – or – y, Dock.

Hot Cross Buns

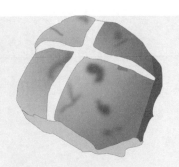
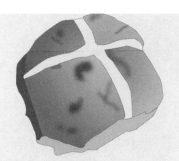

Happy and You Know It

If you're hap – py and you know it clap your hands.

If you're hap – py and you know it clap your hands.

If you're hap – py and you know it, and you

real – ly want to show it. If you're hap – py and you

know it clap your hands.

The Muffin Man

The Mulberry Bush

Sing a Song of Sixpence

Sing a song of six – pence. A poc–ket full of rye.

Four and twen – ty black – birds. Baked in a pie.

When the pie was op – ened the birds be–gan to sing.

Was–n't that a dain–ty dish to set be–fore the king?

22

Row Your Boat

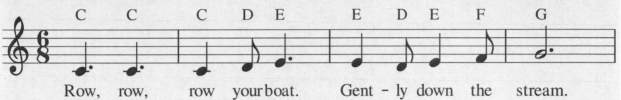

C	C		C	D	E		E	D	E	F		G

Row, row, row your boat. Gent - ly down the stream.

C	C	C	G	G	G		E	E	E	C	C	C		G	F	E	D		C

Merril-y, mer-ril-y, mer-ril-y, mer-ril-y. Life is but a dream.

C	C		C	D	E		E	D	E	F		G

Row, row, row your boat. Gent - ly down the stream.

C	C	G	G	E	E	C		G	F	E	D		C

If you see a cro - co-dile, don't for-get to scream.

Kumbaya

Kum - ba - ya   my   Lord.   Kum - ba - ya.

Kum - ba - ya   my   Lord.   Kum - ba - ya.   Kum - ba - ya   my

Lord.   Kum - ba - ya.   Oh,   Lo - rd,   Kum - ba - ya.

Itsy Bitsy Spider

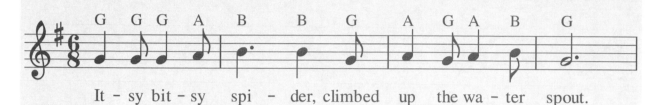

It – sy bit – sy spi – der, climbed up the wa – ter spout.

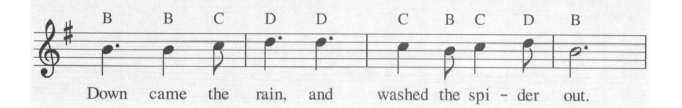

Down came the rain, and washed the spi – der out.

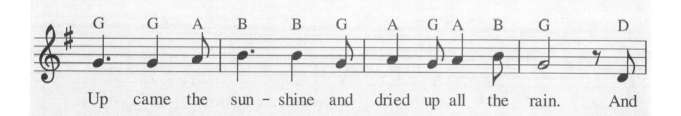

Up came the sun – shine and dried up all the rain. And

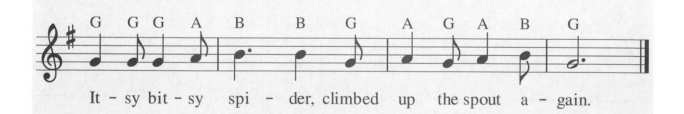

It – sy bit – sy spi – der, climbed up the spout a – gain.

Rudolph the Red-nosed Reindeer

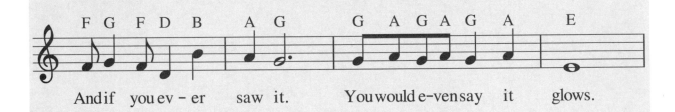

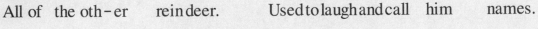

Humpty Dumpty

Hump – ty Dump – ty sat on a wall.

Hump – ty Dump – ty had a great fall.

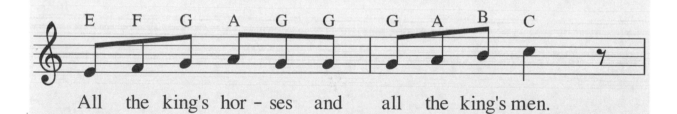

All the king's hor – ses and all the king's men.

Could – n't put Hump – ty to – geth – er a – gain.

Girls and Boys

Girls and boys come out to play. The

moon doth shine as bright as day.

Leave your sup – per and leave your sleep. And

come with your play – fell – ows in – to the street.

Pop Goes the Weasel

Half   a   pound   of   tu – pen – ny   rice.

Half   a   pound   of   trea – cle.   That's   the   way   the

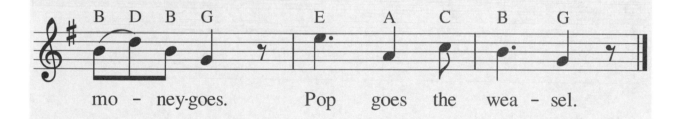

mo – ney·goes.   Pop   goes   the   wea – sel.

Heads, Shoulders, Knees and Toes

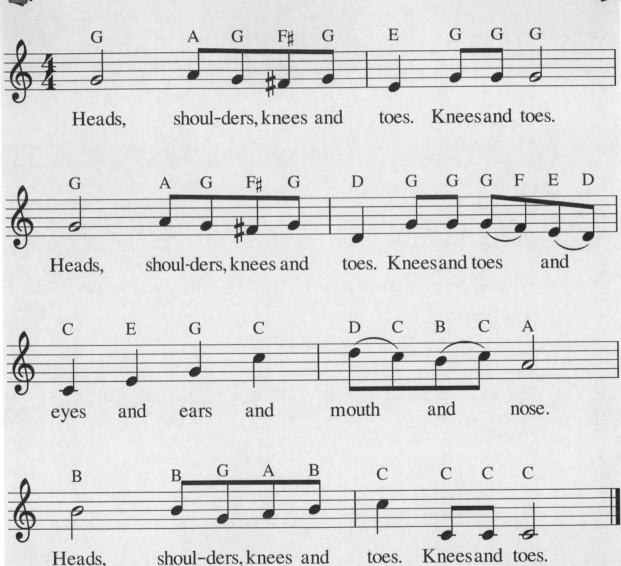

G · A G F♯ G · E · G G G

Heads, · shoul-ders, knees and · toes. · Knees and toes.

G · A G F♯ G · D · G G G F E D

Heads, · shoul-ders, knees and · toes. Knees and toes · and

C E G C · D C B C A

eyes and ears and · mouth and nose.

B · B G A B · C C C C

Heads, · shoul-ders, knees and · toes. Knees and toes.

Nellie the Elephant

Nel-lie the el – e-phant packed her trunk and said goodbye to the

cir – cus. Off she went with a trump – et – y trump.

Trump! Trump! Trump! Nel – lie the el – e-phant

packed her trunk and trun – dled back to the jun – gle.

Off she went with a trumpet – y trump. Trump! Trump! Trump!

Round the Mountain

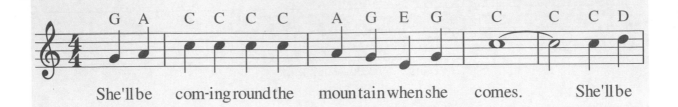

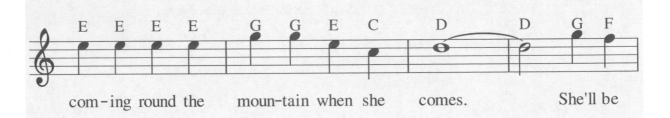

I Am the Music Man

E E E E E G G F G F E

I am the mus-ic man. I come from down the

D G G G A G G G G A G

way. And I can play What can you play?

G G F E C C E E E E E E G F F D

I play the pi-an-o. Pi-a Pi-a Pi-an-o. Pi-an-o.

E E C E E E E E E G F F D B C

Pi-an-o. Pi-a Pi-a Pi-an-o. Pi-a Pi-an-o.

Write Your Own Composition

G - G - f   E - dont

love love me dont

Write Your Own Composition

Write Your Own Composition

Write Your Own Composition

Write Your Own Composition

Write Your Own Composition

Write Your Own Composition